MUTAHHARI IS MUTAHHARI:

THE MAKING OF A THINKER

Mansoor Limba

Contents

Abstract 1

Introduction 3

Statement of the Problem 5

The *Sahifeh-ye Imam* 9

Sahifeh-ye Imam's Account of Mutahhari: A Chronological Survey 19

Sahifeh-ye Imam's Account of Mutahhari: An Analytical Survey 49
  As a trustworthy representative
  As a close associate and confidant
  As a beloved son and student
  As an outstanding author and man of knowledge
  As an eloquent speaker and combatant 'alim
  As a dedicated and pious servant of Islam and the
    nation
  As an epitome of martyrdom and self-sacrifice, and
    reviver of the movement
  As a *furqan* [criterion and acid test]
  As a multi-dimensional figure

Conclusion 63

About the Author 64

Other Books by Mansoor Limba 65

Connect with Mansoor Limba 67

Abstract

A cursory examination of the 22-volume Sahifeh-ye Imam—the largest ever compiled anthology of Imam Khomeini's speeches, messages, interviews, religious decrees, permissions, and letters—reveals that the martyred Ayatullah Professor Murtada Mutahhari undoubtedly occupies a distinct station in the sight of the Great Leader of the Islamic Revolution and the Idol-Breaker of the 20th Century.

Imam Khomeini's communications with Ayatullah Mutahhari in the forms of religious permissions and personal letters, as well as descriptions of him in letters, speeches, messages, statements, interviews, autobiography, and memorial note during and after his lifetime as indicated in the encyclopedic authentic reference source suggest that the former considers the latter a trustworthy representative, compassionate teacher, erudite scholar, competent jurist, eloquent speaker, combatant 'alim, and an epitome of martyrdom in the way of truth and freedom of thought. These benevolent views on him are consistent from the first volume of the anthology in which Professor Mutahhari is indicated having been granted authority [ijazah] on Dhu'l-Hijjah 24, 1388 AHS (March 13, 1969) by the Imam in the financial and religious law affairs up to the 21st volume (volume 22 being the indexes of the whole voluminous treatise) wherein he—in the Imam's message dated Shahrivar 14, 1367 AHS (September 5, 1988) addressed to the Muslim nation of Pakistan and the 'ulama' of Islam on the occasion of the martyrdom of Sayyid 'Arif Husayn Husayni—is mentioned as among "the freedom-loving 'ulama' of the Islamic world subjected to conspiracy and terrorism".

For the Imam, Shahid Mutahhari is more than a student, representative, associate, confidant, friend, or son. Indeed, it can be said that for him, Mutahhari cannot be confined to a single dimension as he is an embodiment of a totality. Mutahhari is Mutahhari.

Introduction

Professor Ayatullah Murtada Mutahhari (1298-1358 AHS) was born on Bahman 13, 1298 AHS [February 3, 1920] in the village of Fariman near Mashhad, Khorasan, to a family of clergymen. His father Hujjat al-Islam Muhammad Husayn Mutahhari was one of the pious *'ulama'* of his time. At the age of 12, after finishing his preliminary education in Fariman, he proceeded to the theological center at Mashhad to receive instruction under Mirza Mahdi Shahidi Radawi.

At the age of 18, he set off for Qum for further pursuits of his studies under the supervision of such great teachers as Ayatullah Burujerdi and Imam Khomeini and others. At this time, he was considered one of the most brilliant students at the theological center of Qum and a favorite student of Imam Khomeini. Beside the philosophy lessons given by Imam Khomeini, the late Mutahhari also attended the Imam's classes on *akhlaq* (ethics). It seems that these lessons had a profound influence in forging his personality. He himself recalls Imam Khomeini's lessons in these words:

> "The lessons in ethics delivered by my beloved and favorite teacher (Imam Khomeini) on every Thursday and Friday were actually exercises and training in treading the spiritual path of gnosticism and were not a dry lesson in lifeless ethics. His teachings overwhelmed me to such an extent that I found myself a great deal under their influence that lasted until the next Monday or Tuesday. A great part of my intellectual and spiritual personality was formed

during those classes which I underwent for 12 years with that spiritual teacher."[1]

Moreover, he himself conducted lessons in subjects like Arabic literature, logic, *kalam* [scholasticism], jurisprudence, and philosophy. In 1331 AHS [1952] Mutahhari was transferred from Qum to Tehran and in 1334 AHS [1955] he was invited to teach Islamic sciences at the Faculty of Islamic Sciences, Tehran University.

He was arrested at the midnight of Khordad 15, 1342 AHS [1963] and spent 43 days in prison. After Imam Khomeini's migration to Paris in France, Mutahhari went to meet him and His Eminence assigned him the responsibility of organizing the Revolutionary Council. On the night of Ordibehesht 11, 1358 AHS [May 1, 1979] Mutahhari was martyred by an agent of the Furqan terrorist group. He wrote more than 50 books and tens of articles, and delivered scores of speeches.

Now, many years after Shahid Mutahhari's martyrdom barely three months after the victory of the Islamic Revolution, it is appropriate to delve on, or review in the least, the different aspects of the noble martyr's personality. As his student at least, what is Imam Khomeini's opinion of Ayatullah Mutahhari? What are the references for these views? Do these views of Mutahhari consistent from the beginning of their acquaintance up to his martyrdom?

---

[1] "Mutahhari's Noble Thoughts Inspiration for Society," *Tehran Times Special Issue on the Martyrdom Anniversary of Ayatullah Mutahhari*, May 1, 1997, p. 3.

Statement of the Problem

Against this backdrop, a critical examination of the viewpoint of the Founder of the Islamic Republic on the late professor in the light of *Sahifeh-ye Imam* is the principal burden of this study.

This paper sought to know the personality of Ayatullah Shaykh Murtada Mutahhari in the words of Imam Khomeini as recorded in *Sahifeh-ye Imam*. In particular, this write up attempted to address the following queries, thus:

1. As the sole reference source of the study, what is *Sahifeh-ye Imam*? To what extent is it reliable as an academic source of inquiry?
2. Chronologically, what are the accounts of *Sahifeh-ye Imam* on Mutahhari?
3. Analytically, what aspects of Mutahhari's personality can be deduced from these chronological accounts of *Sahifeh-ye Imam* on him?

Diagrammatically, this research inquiry can be presented as follows:

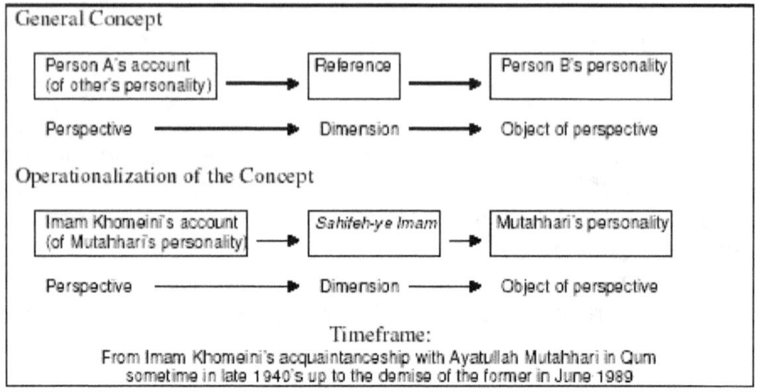

Initially, this paper gave a bird's-eye-view of the *Sahifeh-ye Imam*, the sole source of account of the present analytical survey and examined its academic credibility.

Then, lengthy chronological accounts of the *Sahifeh-ye Imam* on Ayatullah Mutahhari are made. In these accounts only the actual words and writings of Imam Khomeini to, or about, Mutahhari are quoted. Thus, introductory headings in each of the documents, and the footnotes[2] where the former is mentioned—which are not actually parts of the Imam's words and writings, unless otherwise stated—as well as some instances[3] in the text where his name is only mentioned without the Imam having elaborating on his personality are not covered. Equally excluded is Volume 22 of

---

[2] For instance, *Sahifeh-ye Imam: Majmu'eh-ye Athar-e Imam Khomeini (Bayyanat, Payam, Musahebeh-ha, Ahkam, Ijazat-e Shar'i, Nameh-ha) (Sahifeh-ye Imam*: An Anthology of Imam Khomeini's Speeches, Messages, Interviews, Decrees, Permissions, and Letters) (Tehran: The Institute for Compilation and Publication of Imam Khomeini's Works, Autumn 1378 AHS), vol. 1, p. 410; vol. 21, p. 461; vol. 15, p. 174. Hereafter, the anthology will be only cited as "*Sahifeh-ye Imam*".

[3] For instance, it can be cited the mentioning of "Mutahhari Madrasah," which has nothing to do directly with the personality of the Martyr. *Sahifeh-ye Imam*, vol. 14, pp. 168-169.

the *Sahifeh* being the comprehensive index of the encyclopedic work.

Thereafter, an analysis of the chronological accounts is conducted to arrive at an overall picture of Ayatullah Mutahhari in the words of Imam Khomeini. In the conclusion, the findings of the study, which are actually the restatement of the answers to the points of clarification, are stated.

The *Sahifeh-ye Imam*

Published by the Tehran-based Institute for the Compilation and Publication of Imam Khomeini's Works (ICPIKW) in the year 1378 AHS (1999) named as the "Year of Imam Khomeini" being the centennial year of his birth, the *Sahifeh-ye Imam* has been so far the largest anthology of Imam Khomeini's literary works including his family-related letters, religious permissions, socio-political letters and telegrams, decrees and orders, messages, speeches and statements, interviews and dialogues, and others.

The family-related letters open an impressive window on the private life of the Imam. These letters show that not only was Imam an ideal role model in the realms of scholarship and *ijtihad*, struggle and *jihad*, and politics and leadership for his disciples, but also his subtle soul and his self-disciplined and dutiful personality urged him not to shirk his duties in the non-political spheres. He was an idyllic spouse in his conjugal behavior and in terms of gentleness and fidelity toward his wife. As both his quest and fate led him to Ayatullah Thaqafi's home to select his partner for all his sorrows and ecstasies, he remained committed to this first and last selected one to the end of life and along all its ups and downs. A departure for the obligatory *hajj* pilgrimage in his youth, a year of exile to Turkey and a few trips of his wife to Iran for visiting the children and relatives (during the joint sojourn in the holy city of Najaf, Iraq) were the few cases, during the 60 years of married life when he and his wife experienced separation. The archive of surviving letters displays a deep, emotional and loyal relationship replete with affection and mutual respect. The letters of Imam Khomeini to his children and relatives show us another aspect of a great soul, and it is that being a Religious Reference Authority [(Source of Imitation) *marja' at-taqlid*] and a religious patriarch and dealing with the leadership of the Revolution made him considerate of the religious and moral duties regarding his relatives and children. The Imam's training strategy toward the children and his granting them the right to choose and free will along with compassionate supervision can all be observed in these writings.[4]

Imam Khomeini's letters of authorization to a choice of people in the financial and religious law [*shar'iyyah* wa *hasbiyyah*] affairs, either chosen by himself or in response to individual requests for authorization, form another part of *Sahifeh-ye Imam*. According to the principles of Shi'ah jurisprudence [*fiqh*], any expenditure of the religious payments and management of the Islamic financial affairs during the period of occultation of the twelfth Imam is not authorized without the permission of a fully qualified jurist; so it has been customary for the *maraji' at-taqlid* to issue letters of authorization for the qualified persons. The faithful pay their religious dues through these representatives to their *maraji'*. The issued authorizations indicate the scope of authority of the recipient of the permission for expending the payments in the lawful religious ways. These authorizations are granted to persons who meet the criteria of authority of imitation [*marja'iyyah*] in terms of general qualifications, devoutness and commitment, or their qualification is certified by two just informed persons. We can conclude from the collection of authorizations issued by Imam Khomeini and particularly from the letters written by His Eminence to his official representatives that he has been diligent and scrupulous in issuing the permissions. Except the cases of authorizations that have been issued for the prominent and pious scholars or for the persons who were closely in contact with and known to him, generally Imam has not issued any authorizations without a written endorsement of the just informed persons. An index of the religious authorizations issued by Imam Khomeini during the period of his stay in the holy city of Najaf is included at the end of this volume (volume one) of *Sahifeh-ye Imam*. The original copy of this index is available in Imam's handwriting and it demonstrates the Imam's fastidiousness and organization in such cases. It should be mentioned that the religious authorizations are only valid as long as the

---

[4] *Sahifeh-ye Imam*, vol. 1, p. xxi.

beneficiary remains virtuous, and possesses the other attributes required for being the lawful representative in collecting and expending the religious payments, otherwise they will be automatically dismissed. In the present collection, only the authorizations are included of which a certified copy has been available, while the number of the religious permissions granted by Imam Khomeini exceed this.[5]

Another component of *Sahifeh-ye Imam* is the telegrams and letters written by Imam Khomeini to different persons, religious scholars, local and foreign diplomats and political leaders, various political parties and societies, and ordinary people, which embrace a variety of themes. The diverse addressees of these letters and the vast span of time that they cover, beside the variety of their themes and subjects, all add to the significance of these letters as a part of the wealth of documents that relate fragments of the history of the Imam's movement and His Eminence' positions and views on different issues. Among these letters, we cross upon records that have instigated some developments in the course of the uprising and during the Islamic Revolution. For example, the Imam's telegrams and letters to the Shah, Asadullah 'Alam and Amir-'Abbas Hoveyda, as well as his letters to the *maraji' at-taqlid*, *'ulama*, seminaries, political and religious associations in the country and abroad, and leaders of foreign states. Fortunately, through the efforts made by the Imam's Memento (Haj Sayyid Ahmad Khomeini) (*r*),[6] the original manuscripts of many of Imam Khomeini's letters and telegrams since the climax of the Islamic Revolution in 1356 AHS 1978] till his demise has been collected and are available in the Institute. Moreover, through the efforts of the Institute and the assistance of his friends, a great deal of Imam Khomeini's correspondence in the years preceding the victory of the Islamic Revolution has been recovered, all of which together with the other works and records of His

---

[5] *Ibid.*, pp. xxii-xxiii.

[6] The abbreviation, "*r*" stands for the Arabic invocative phrase, *rahmatullah 'alayh, rahmatullah 'alayha,* or *rahmatullah 'alayhim* [may God have mercy on him/her/them], which is used after the names of pious people.

Eminence are thereby published, with no alterations, in *Sahifeh-ye Imam*.[7]

A large number of decrees and orders of His Eminence Imam Khomeini, as the *marja'* of many of the Shi'ah people and as the Great Leader of the Revolution and the Islamic Republic of Iran have survived, which are exactly printed in the collection. The decrees published in *Sahifeh-ye Imam* include those issued for the formation of the Revolutionary Council, the transitional government and appointment of its members; confirmation of the Constitution; approval of the presidential decrees; decrees on the foundation of different revolutionary institutions; decrees for installing and deposing the judiciary, military, and law enforcement officials, and the Leader's representatives in various institutions and organizations; the military orders issued by him as the Commander-in-Chief of the Armed Forces, as well as His Eminence's directives and orders issued response to the requests of government officials on diverse issues. Studying this part of the Imam's works, especially observing the historical trend they have taken along with His Eminence's messages and speeches, offers an overall view of the kind of his religious and proficient, decisive and potent leadership and yet, unassuming and people-based. Since some of Imam Khomeini's views and orders have been written at the bottom of request letters of officials and inquirers, all or parts of the original requests are published together with the Imam's response for a better understanding of the issue.[8]

Imam Khomeini's different religious and political messages comprise some of the most important written works of Imam Khomeini collected and chronologically published in *Sahifeh-ye Imam*. Issuing and publishing these messages was in fact the most important direct channel through which Imam Khomeini kept in touch with the people and his followers. It was via these messages that, during the Provincial and District Councils Bill affair, the rising surge against the monarchial regime began and the Khordad 15,

---

[7] *Sahifeh-ye Imam*, vol. pp. xxiii-xxiv.
[8] *Ibid.*, pp. xxiv-xxv.

1342 AHS [June 5, 1963] uprising started. All along the struggles of the Iranian nation, they were Imam's statements and messages that determined the method of uprising, the rational and political bases, and its main concerns, slogans and approaches in each of the strenuous stages of the Revolution. When in 1356 and 1357 AHS [1977 and 1978] the Iranian nation's struggle was heightening, each statement issued by Imam Khomeini from Najaf (in Iraq) or Paris, which swiftly circulated all around the country, stood for a general and national manifesto that determined the course of the Revolution, and organized the revolutionary forces and the people around certain objectives and maxims. In his messages, Imam Khomeini did not just aim at invoking the heroic spirits and encouraging the people to steadfastness and persistence on the course of the Revolution. Rather, His Eminence, with his versatile and lucid writing style, tried to increase the public religious and political awareness regarding the current affairs, and to augment their insight concerning the proponents and opponents of the Revolution inside the country and abroad, so that they might be encouraged consciously to get involved in supporting the objectives of the Revolution. The themes most conspicuous in Imam Khomeini's statements include wisely foreseeing the schemes designed by the Shah's regime and its Western supporters for suppressing the uprising at each stage and making the effort to thwart them, warning against the misleading slogans and positions in the course of the struggle, and highly stressing the public concurrence over their shared religious slogans. What was common in all of Imam Khomeini's messages, both before and after the victory of the Revolution, was calling the people to supporting the goals of the Revolution from the perspective of the religious and divine duty, and with reliance on the people's role as the primary founders and owners of the Revolution, with an exceptional emphasis on the youth.[9]

A key element in Imam Khomeini's successful management and leadership was his extensive relationship with the masses and various strata of society. The complex

---

[9] *Ibid.*, pp. xxv-xxvii.

link between realities and ideals, and the establishment of relationship between theory and practice show the sagacious obvious image of his leadership. Great theoreticians and idealists have seldom attained their ideals. He did not merely depend on the scientific and practical treatises in presenting and propagating his religious-political ideals, and this is what made him a rare or even unique in the annals of religious authority [*marja'iyyah*]. Just as he occupied a lofty position as a great religious authority among his followers, he could be able to explain in plain language deep religious concepts particularly the political and social aspects of religion to his audience. Imam Khomeini's numerous messages at the gathering of various strata of the people provided the possibility of direct connection of the people with his ideas and views, and made them needless of the official and unofficial interpretations of intermediaries, which are mostly associated with the exercise of their personal views and political and factional motives. Contextual analysis of the Imam's speeches and his knowledge of the audience, and a comparison of the historical events of the Islamic Revolution with the trend of his speeches and statements, and the study of the aggregate of meetings and speeches, and the diversity of the groups and strata will help the researchers in analyzing the realities of the Islamic Revolution and in finding the reason behind Imam Khomeini's effective and people based-leadership. For this reason, in compiling the Imam's speeches and their publication in *Sahifeh-ye Imam* no literary or textual edition, or change of any type, which is quite usual in the process of rendering speeches into publishable written text has been undertaken. Given that these speeches of Imam Khomeini were delivered in relation to the historical events of the Islamic Revolution with the trend of his speeches and statements, and the study of the aggregate of meetings and speeches, and the diversity of the groups and strata will help the researchers in analyzing the realities of the Islamic Revolution and in finding the reason behind Imam Khomeini's effective and people based-leadership.[10]

---

[10] *Ibid.*, pp. xxviii-xxx.

In the age of communications, the mass media's interviews with the intellectual and political leaders with the aim of elucidating their viewpoints, and dispel ambiguities and enigmas through answering the reporters' questions, is one of the effective means of establishing communication and direction in the public opinion. Being aware of the importance of this phenomenon and in the absence of restrictions, Imam Khomeini granted unconditional audience to journalists and pressmen. The best part of his interviews took place during his sojourn in Paris. As a result, the numerous interviews by the leading world news agencies, radio-TV networks of various countries, and Iranian and foreign newspapers and periodicals with Imam Khomeini, and his concise yet categorical and well-reasoned out answers to the questions have become part of the compendium of the Imam's valuable socio-political works, which in the present work have been presented to the esteemed readers. The Imam's talks with state leaders and their envoys have so many instructive points. Examples are his reception of the Elysee Palace's envoys during his stay in Paris; holding talks with mediators of the American government; his type of treatment and statements in his first meeting with the ex-USSR's ambassador; his meeting with Yasir 'Arafat and Palestinian leaders; and his meeting with Edward Shevardnadze as Gorbachev's special envoy who carried the latter's reply to Imam Khomeini's famous message;[11] dialogue with leaders of the Muslim countries and other foreign political figures—which from the point of view of the statement of the two sides and the extremely simple and unbelievable reception—and the Imam's self-confidence and proficiency in the arena of discussion are among the different informative aspects for the Third World statesmen and leaders particularly that of the Islamic Republic. Certainly, such disposition and style of Imam Khomeini have multiplied a hundred times the Iranian

---

[11] See *A Call to Divine Unity: Letter of Imam Khomeini, the Great Leader of the Islamic Revolution and Founder of the Islamic Republic of Iran, to Mikhail Gorbachev, Leader of the Soviet Union,* 2nd ed. (Tehran: The Institute for Compilation and Publication of Imam Khomeini's Works, 2003).

nation's sense of identity and self-confidence in the arenas of confronting the formidable enemies of the Revolution and in defending the Islamic country.[12]

So far, Imam Khomeini's speeches and messages have been published in hundreds of works under various titles and styles (summarized or complete, thematically or chronologically) in manifold languages by his devotees and cultural institutions both inside and outside Iran. Imam's devotees and the cultural institutes accomplished this both within and without Iran. Undoubtedly, these works particularly his socio-political works are among the published works with the highest circulation in Farsi language. Among the published books from Imam Khomeini's general works (before the establishment of this Institute), some have been outstanding. Despite the demerits and defects which can be seen and have been the point of some criticisms in *Sahifeh-ye Nur*, it should be stated that this work from the time of publication of its first volume up to now has so far been the most comprehensive reference for the researchers and those interested in the works of Imam Khomeini. Worthy of acknowledgment are the valuable efforts and endeavor of the compilers of *Sahifeh-ye Nur* from the Ministry of Culture and Islamic Guidance, and the Organization of Islamic Revolution's Cultural Documents, and the dear ones who have rendered valuable assistance in the different stages of compilation and publication of this work for all those who have benefited from this pathway to the treasure of the Imam's literary works in their research, seminars, speeches, and references. Among the merits of *Sahifeh-ye Nur* are its lengthy introduction by Ayatullah, lucid titles, chronological arrangement, table of contents, skillful editing, as well as relative comprehensiveness. In a bid to present a complete series of all the literary works of Imam Khomeini and keeping in view the main shortcomings and defects existing in the *Sahifeh-ye Nur*, the Institute has published the present work entitled, *Sahifeh-ye Imam*. During many years in the different department of this Institute, the existing texts in the *Sahifeh-ye Nur*, newspapers, periodicals, and books have

---

[12] *Sahifeh-ye Imam*, vol. 1, pp. xxx, xxxiii.

been collated with the cassette recorded tapes, handwritings and original manuscripts of Imam Khomeini's works which are at the disposal of the Institute, and the final text is meticulously selected. All the date inconsistencies and other defects existing in the *Sahifeh-ye Nur* and other sources concerning the identification of each of the Imam's works have been investigated, and the authentic and final facts have been presented at the beginning of each piece of work along with its identification (headings). Apart from the mentioned points, the most important merit of the *Sahifeh-ye Imam* over the *Sahifeh-ye Nur* and other published books on the Imam's works is the inclusion of over 2,000 cases of his works and documents from among the unpublished works of the Imam, which become available for the public for the first time. The meticulous selection of the indices (proper names, subjects and terms, Qur'anic verses and *hadith*s, etc.) and their presentation in one volume (volume 22), which provides easy access to selected topics and subjects of the first 21 volumes.[13]

From the above scrutiny of the *Sahifeh-ye Imam*, it becomes clear that it has so far been the most comprehensive and reliable collection of Imam Khomeini's literary works. So, it is only proper to take this anthology as the sole reference in objectively examining the personality of Ayatullah Mutahhari in the light of Imam Khomeini's written communication with, and views on, him.

---

[13] *Ibid.*, pp. xxxiii-xxxvi. For information on the Imam's works not published in the anthology, see *Sahifeh-ye Imam*, vol. 1, pp. xxxvi-xxxix.

Sahifeh-ye Imam's Account of Mutahhari:
A Chronological Survey

In the first volume of the anthology, Ayatullah Mutahhari is included in the Imam's personal list of individuals he, in capacity of being a *marja' at-taqlid*, has granted permission [*ijazah*] in the financial and religious law affairs:

334. To: Hujjat al-Islam Mr. Haj Shaykh Murtada Mutahhari Khorasani, in Tehran
Recommender: Renowned
Scope of Authority: Financial; delivering a half
Date: Dhu'l-Hijjah 1388 AH[14]

In the second volume, we can find the permission itself dated March 11, 1969 [Esfand 20, 1347 AHS/Dhu'l-Hijjah 24, 1388 AH] granted by the Imam during his exile in Najaf, Iraq. The text of the permission is as follows:

In the Name of God, the Compassionate, the Merciful

Praise be to Allah, Lord of the worlds; may peace and salutations be upon Muhammad and his pure progeny; and may Allah's curse be upon all their enemies.

His Eminence 'Imad al-'Ulama' wa Hujjat al-Islam Mr. Haj Shaykh Murtada Mutahhari, may his graces last, has been granted my permission to be in charge of the financial and religious law affairs whose supervision depends on the permission of a fully-qualified jurist during the occultation of *Wali al-Amr*, may Allah expedite his glorious advent, "so that he will be in charge of the mentioned affairs while exercising caution." He is also authorized to collect the blessed Share of the Imam (*'a*) and spend one-half of it in

---

[14] *Sahifeh-ye Imam*, vol. 1, p. 488.

such cases as are beneficial for the exaltation of Islam, the promotion of the sacred precepts, and the elevation of the foundation of the sacred religion; and to remit the other half to this humble being to be spent at the significant religious seminaries. He is also empowered to have funds change hands, allow grace periods as deemed necessary and in collecting, spending and remitting in the manner mentioned above.

"And I advise him, may God, the Exalted, assist him, as we have been advised by the pious predecessors to keep company of piety, to evade carnal desires, and to be meticulous in his worldly and afterworld affairs. I hope he will not forget me in his benevolent prayers." May God's peace, mercy and blessings be upon him and our pious brethren.

Ruhullah al-Musawi al-Khomeini
Dhu'l-Hijjah al-Haram 24, 1388 AH[15]

In the same volume, while still in exile in Najaf, Iraq, the Imam extends the following letter of condolence dated March 5, 1972 [Esfand 10, 1350 AHS / Muharram 13, 1391 AH] to Shahid Mutahhari on the occasion of his father's demise:

In His Most Exalted Name

Muharram al-Haram 13, 1392 AH

His Eminence 'Imad al-A'lam wa Hujjat al-Islam Mr. Mutahhari, may his graces last:

As it was reported from the Holy City of Mecca the late Hujjat al-Islam, your father, may God have mercy on him, returned to the Mercy of the Lord. I pray to God, the Exalted, for a lofty station for him, and patience and recompense for you and the rest of your family. I had a special affection to him. "As what God, the Exalted wants, we will return to Him." I hope for benevolent prayers from you. May peace be upon you.

---

[15] *Sahifeh-ye Imam*, vol. 2, p. 221.

Ruhullah al-Musawi al-Khomeini[16]

Around January to March 1978 [the end of 1356 AHS/the beginning of 1398 AH], in his place of banishment in Najaf the Imam sent a personal letter to Professor Mutahhari, who was then in Tehran, concerning the deplorable state of the Islamic seminaries at that time, as thus recorded in volume three of the *Sahifeh*:

In His Most Exalted Name

After extending my greetings and best wishes to you, I would like to say that I have received your esteemed letter and that I pray for your honor's health and prosperity. Most of the topics that have been mentioned were and are under consideration. It is hoped that the efforts to prevent mischief will meet with success. As you are far away from the Qum Seminary and so are some of the other gentlemen—it being better if their services are availed of in these chaotic conditions and turmoil—these expected evils are the cause of my anxiety. The people you have mentioned cannot solve this problem if not adding to it because of the intervention of some, the likes of which have upset the youth. The case of the council and a meeting of arbiters for solving and settling the problem will also not solve any difficulty. In fact, such a meeting will not materialize. I have experience; as a matter of fact, much experience. That which tops the mischief list is the very same third case to which you have referred as threatening the seminary from within. It should be reminded, and there is no remedy except that the gentlemen who are acceptable and who, with respect to knowledge, can be provided, stay in the seminaries and take hold of the initiative. You are in a better position to select these people, and you can find people who can stay in the seminaries on all days— even if it be in turns—and gradually exert an influence on the morale of the youths.

---

[16] *Ibid.*, p. 424.

21

In my recent, detailed letter, written in answer to that of the Union of Islamic Associations in Europe,[17] I have explained the main problems and shown the way, pointing out the evil of this perverted conviction that the religious sciences, as also modern education, are worthless. Perhaps, opportunity arising, I will comment on this matter in a message to the Qum Seminary. But just pointing it out is not enough; these digressions must be prevented in practice. This should be accomplished by the efforts of the concerned notables including yourself.

It is hoped that the honorable gentlemen who have taken notice of the matter by the grace of God, and have changed their attitude somewhat, will be favored by the support of all the various groups, and that the disputes and differences will be eliminated or, at least, narrowed.[18]

All the above quotations constitute the Imam's direct communications with the martyred professor. The ensuing volumes reflect what the Great Leader of the Islamic Revolution says about him. It starts with the message to the Iranian nation released by the Imam on May 1, 1979 [Ordibehesht 11, 1358 AHS/Jamadi ath-Thani 4, 1399 AH] on the occasion of the martyrdom of Murtada Mutahhari. Extolling the personality and academic standing of the Martyr, the message runs as follows:

In the Name of God, the Compassionate, the Merciful
"Verily to Allah we belong and to Him we shall return."

I express my condolences and congratulations to Islam, to its exalted prophets, to the nation of Islam and in particular, to the combatant people of Iran for the sorrowful loss of the honorable martyr, thinker, philosopher, and esteemed *faqih* [jurist] the late Haj Shaykh Murtada Mutahhari—may his soul rest in peace. Condolence on the

---

[17] It refers to Imam's message of Rabi' al-Awwal 5, 1398 AH [11/24/1356 AHS] to the Union of Islamic Associations of Students in Europe.

[18] *Sahifeh-ye Imam*, vol. 3, p. 328.

martyrdom of a personage who spent his noble and precious life in the cause of the sacred objectives of Islam and who struggled ferociously with deviations and perversions; condolences on the martyrdom of a man who was peerless in Islamology and various Islamic studies and the glorious Qur'an studies. I have lost a very beloved son and mourn for him, for he was among the personalities that were considered to be the achievement of my life. With the martyrdom of this honorable son and immortal scholar, in a blow has been dealt beloved Islam that nothing can substitute. And felicitations on the possession of these self-sacrificing personalities who spread and are spreading light with their appearance, both in this life and the hereafter. I congratulate the great Islam, the trainer of human beings and the Islamic nation for rearing such offspring, who with their luminous light give life to the dead and spread light in darkness. Although I have lost a beloved child who was a part of my being, I am honored that such self-sacrificing children had existed and exist in Islam. Mutahhari who was peerless in purity of soul and strength of faith and the power of oratory, has departed and joined the ranks of the exalted souls, but the malevolent people should know that with his departure, his Islamic, scholarly, and philosophical personality has not gone.

Terrorists cannot assassinate the humane personality of the men of Islam. They should know that by the will of the powerful God, with the departure of great individuals our nation will become more determined in its resolve to fight against immorality, tyranny, and oppression. Our nation has found its way and now will not rest until the obliteration of the decayed roots of the former regime and its evil supporters. The beloved Islam proliferated with the sacrifice and martyrdom of its most beloved ones. From the age of revelation until now, Islam has thrived on martyrdom interlaced with moral heroism. Fighting for the cause of God and the cause of the downtrodden has been at the head of Islam's plans. *"Why do you not fight in the way of Allah and for the sake of weak men and women and children?"*[19]

---

[19] *Sūrah an-Nisa' 5:75.*

These people, who have tasted their defeat and death and by means of this inhuman behavior wish to take revenge or in their own wishful thinking, frighten the holy warriors of Islam are wrong in their thinking. From every strand of hair of a martyr from us; and from every drop of blood that pours to the ground, determined and combatant human beings are created. Unless you assassinate the whole courageous nation, the assassination of a single individual; however, great he may be, will be of no benefit for returning to your plundering. A nation that with trust in the great God and for the revival of Islam, has risen, will not turn around by these desperate attempts. We are ready for sacrifice and are prepared for martyrdom in the cause of God.

I announce Thursday, May 3, 1979, as a day of public mourning for paying respects to a self-sacrificing and holy warrior of the path of Islam and the nation; and I shall be in mourning on Thursday and Friday at the Faydiyyah Madrasah. I implore the Almighty God to grant blessings and forgiveness to that beloved son of Islam, and honor and glory to Islam. Salutations to the martyrs of the path of truth and freedom.

Ruhullah al-Musawi al-Khomeini[20]

On the third-day commemoration and mourning ceremony of Mutahhari's martyrdom [May 4, 1979/Ordibehesht 14, 1358 AHS/Jamadi ath-Thani 7, 1399 AH], in his speech delivered at the Faydiyyah Madrasah to the various strata of the people, the Imam has this to say on the role of his martyrdom in strengthening the Islamic Revolution:

Our movement was resurrected. All sections of the people of Iran started life all over again. If it had developed lethargy or a weakness, it was resurrected. Was it not because of the martyrdom of this great man; and had this great man died in his bed; this would not have been

---

[20] *Sahifeh-ye Imam*, vol. 7, pp. 178-179.

substantiated; this wave would not have arisen. Now a wave, all over the world; the entire world; all the world that is interested in Islam has arisen. My brothers in the rest of the countries be not afraid of this wave.[21]

The subsequent part of the volume (volume 7) is full of the Imam's acknowledgment of gratitude in the form of letters, messages and statements for the messages of condolence he received from various personalities both from inside and outside Iran. We have, for example, the following lines:

In His Most Exalted Name

Jamadi ath-Thani 9, 1399 AH

His Eminence Sayyid al-A'lam wa Thiqat al-Islam Mr. Sayyid Muhammad Khatami, may his blessings last:
I received your telegram of condolence for the sorrowful martyrdom of the late Hujjat al-Islam wal-Muslimin Mr. Mutahhari—may his soul be sanctified—for which I thank you. Other telegrams on this occasion were also received from the Islamic Association of Students in Europe and the Iranians resident in Germany, Britain, France, and other European countries. You kindly requested to convey my deep gratitude and greetings to all of them. I pray to Almighty God for everyone's success. May God's peace, mercy, and blessings be upon you.

Ruhullah al-Musawi al-Khomeini[22]

I would like to thank you for the communication of condolences on behalf of the President, government and the people of your country with regard to this great tragedy that has befallen us and our country—rather to the nation of Islam.

---

[21] *Ibid.*, p. 183-184.
[22] Letter dated May 6, 1979 [Ordibehesht 16, 1358 AHS / Jamadi ath-Thani 9, 1399 AH]. *Ibid.*, p. 194.

Nevertheless, we must give such martyrs, for the cause of Islam. From day one when Islam was born, it has propagated this righteous religion with martyrdom. Islam has had great martyrs and it is honored to have given great martyrs in the way of God and in the path of its objective. We too are honored to give martyrs in the cause of Islam and in the path of our objective—and this man is not the last of our martyrs. We may again have to give martyrs; and for us the life of this world is inconsequential. The objective is important and we shall strive in the path of the objective. And whatever happens in this regard we welcome it because it is for the attainment of the objective.[23]

In the Name of God, the Compassionate, the Merciful

His Excellency Colonel Mu'ammar Qadhdhafi, President of Libya:

I received the telegram of condolence of Your Excellency, which was transmitted on the sorrowful martyrdom of the late Hujjat al-Islam wal-Muslimin Professor Mutahhari. I thank you for the expression of your sympathy. The martyrdom of one of the greatest scholars of Islam was a loss for the world of Islam and all the Muslims. And our enemies have once again proven their antagonism and hostility towards Islam and the Muslims but they are ignorant of the fact that these desperate attempts make our Muslim and the awakened nation more determined to tread this path, and these satanic plots can never stop them in their path. I pray to the Almighty God for the success and happiness of all Muslims.

Ruhullah al-Musawi al-Khomeini[24]

---

[23] Statements given in Qum on May 7, 1979 [Ordibehesht 17, 1358 AHS / Jamadi ath-Thani 10, 1399 AH] to the Ambassador of Somalia. *Ibid.*, p. 197.

[24] Message issued in Qum on May 8, 1979 [Ordibehesht 18, 1358 AHS / Jamadi ath-Thani 11, 1399 AH]. *Ibid.*, p. 202.

Then, on a single day, the Imam had to reply to four separate messages of condolence from various parts of Iran:

In His Most Exalted Name

Jamadi ath-Thani 12, 1399 AH

Jahrum

His Eminence Hujjat al-Islam wal-Muslimin Haj Sayyid Ibrahim Haqqshenas, may his blessings last:

I received the telegram of condolence on your behalf and that of the rest of the sections of the respected residents of Jahrum on the sorrowful martyrdom of the late Hujjat al-Islam wal-Muslimin Professor Murtada Mutahhari—may his soul rest in peace.

I thank the gentlemen for their expression of sympathy, and pray to God the Almighty for the success of all of you. May peace, mercy, and blessings of Allah be upon you.

Ruhullah al-Musawi al-Khomeini[25]

In His Most Exalted Name

Jamadi ath-Thani 12, 1399 AH

His Eminence Hujjat al-Islam wal-Muslimin Haj Shaykh 'Ali Ansari, may his blessings last:

The telegram of the condolence on your behalf, the rest of the religious scholars and the various strata of the people of Ahwaz on the sorrowful martyrdom of the late Hujjat al-Islam wal-Muslimin Professor Murtada Mutahhari has been received. Convey my sincere thanks and best wishes to all the gentlemen and especially to your respected nephews. I

---

[25] Letter dated May 9, 1979 [Ordibehesht 19, 1358 AHS / Jamadi ath-Thani 12, 1399 AH]. *Ibid.*, p. 207.

pray to God for the success and happiness of all of you. May God's peace, mercy, and blessings be upon you.

Ruhullah al-Musawi al-Khomeini[26]

In His Most Exalted Name

Jamadi ath-Thani 12, 1399 AH

Ordibehesht 19, 1358 AHS

His Eminence Hujjat al-Islam wal-Muslimin Haj 'Ata'ullah Ashrafi Isfahani, may his blessings last:

I acknowledge the receipt of the telegram message on your behalf and that of the rest of the religious scholars of Kermanshah—may their blessings last long—regarding condolence on the martyrdom of the late Hujjat al-Islam wal-Muslimin Professor Mutahhari Murtada—may his soul be sanctified I thank you gentlemen for your expression of sympathy. I pray to the Almighty God for the success and happiness of all of you in the path of service to Islam and the Muslims. May peace, mercy, and blessings of Allah be upon you.

Ruhullah al-Musawi al-Khomeini[27]

In His Most Exalted Name

Jamadi ath-Thani 12, 1399 AH

His Eminence Hujjat al-Islam Mr. Afqahi Sabzevari, may his blessings last:

---

[26] Letter dated May 9, 1979 [Ordibehesht 19, 1358 AHS / Jamadi ath-Thani 12, 1399 AH]. *Ibid.*, p. 208.
[27] Letter dated May 9, 1979. *Ibid.*, p. 209.

I acknowledge the receipt of your telegram message regarding condolence for the martyrdom of the late Hujjat al-Islam wal-Muslimin Professor Mutahhari—may his soul be sanctified. I thank you for your expression of sympathy. I pray to the Almighty God for the success and happiness of you. May God's peace, mercy, and blessings be upon you.

Ruhullah al-Musawi al-Khomeini[28]

In a speech in Qum addressed to a group of students of the Medical University of Tehran on the same day (May 9, 1979), the Imam explained the impact of Mutahhari's martyrdom, hence:

... we must not be in the least anxious that our people are being killed. This Islam has been founded in this manner right from its inception and it has marched forward while giving martyrs; it has constantly given martyrs and moved forward. It was the same in the era of the Holy Prophet too. In the Battle of Uhud,[29] so many people were killed and in the other battles, so many Muslims were killed but they were not worried at all. They would give martyrs and move one step forward; again, they would give martyrs and move one step forward; And, praise be to God, now the situation is such that by giving a single martyr an upsurge is created all over Iran and outside Iran. Outside Iran also, the incident of the death of the late Mr. Mutahhari—which justifiably was a great loss for us and for the whole of Iran—as you are aware was a loss too, they broadcast on the radio stations that in Pakistan or in such and

---

[28] Letter dated May 9, 1979 [Ordibehesht 19, 1358 AHS / Jamadi ath-Thani 12, 1399 AH]. *Ibid.*, p. 210.

[29] Uhud is the name of a mountain near the city of Medina in the Arabian Peninsula. One of the battles between the Holy Prophet (*s*) and the polytheists took place near the said mountain in 3 AH. During the battle, Hamzah, the Prophet's uncle along with 70 other Muslims were martyred. The reason for this defeat was the Muslims' failure to heed the Prophet's instructions in their greed to get war booties.

29

such place—everywhere—it has created a wave. These people too are making a mistake by killing Mr. Mutahhari. They must understand that the question is not that with the killing of a single person the people will retreat, when one is killed the whole lot comes forward and their cry becomes louder; the disgrace of the enemy also becomes more. And I hope that this spirit stays with us and with our nation.[30]

In another speech on May 10, 1979 [Ordibehesht 20, 1358 AHS / Jamadi ath-Thani 13, 1399 AH] on the same occasion of the martyrdom of Mutahhari, the Imam emphasized on martyrdom being an eternal honor to a group of the Air Force personnel of Tehran, students of the Intermediate Teachers' College of Isfahan; group of teachers; Kalhor tribes of the border areas; trainees of the National Oil Company of Abadan; students of the women's Elementary Teachers' College of Abadeh; Women of Husayniyyah al-Irshad; and Employees of the Meat Organization:

Today, that you have gathered here to express your condolences on the death of one of our beloved, and for the assassination of a scholar, knowingly and determinedly you are resolved to continue the struggle against the *taghuti*[31] regime, colonialism, and arrogance. My brothers! My sisters! My dear ones! Be resolute, do not be afraid of assassination; do not be afraid of martyrdom, and for sure you are not. Martyrdom is an eternal honor; it is immortality. Those people should be afraid of martyrdom and be afraid of death who regard death to be the end and human beings to be ephemeral. Whereas why should we, who regard human beings to be immortal and the eternal life to be better than this worldly life, be afraid? I thank all the various sections of the people, the tribes, the army personnel, the ladies and the teachers, who have gathered together here, and pray to

---

[30] *Sahifeh-ye Imam*, pp. 219-220.

[31] *Ṭāghūt*: a term which has been used eight times in the Qur'an and refers to one who surpasses all bounds in his despotism and tyranny and claims the prerogatives of divinity for himself whether explicitly or implicitly.

the Blessed and Almighty God for the health and happiness of all.[32]

On May 11-12, 1979, the Imam replied to two more condolence messages on the martyrdom of Mutahhari:

In His Most Exalted Name

Jamadi ath-Thani 14, 1399 AH

His Eminence Hujjat al-Islam Haj Sayyid Mahdi Yathribi—may his blessings last:
Your telegram and that of the Association of Clergymen of Kashan on the occasion of the sorrowful martyrdom of the late Hujjat al-Islam wal-Muslimin Professor Mutahhari—may his soul be sanctified—has been received. Please send my sincere thanks and greetings to all the respected gentlemen.
I pray to the Blessed and Almighty God for the success of all in the cause of service to Islam and the Muslims. May God's peace, mercy, and blessings be upon you.

Ruhullah al-Musawi al-Khomeini[33]

In His Most Exalted Name

Your Majesty Shaykh Zayid bin Sultan Al-i Nahyan—Head of the United Arab Emirates:
The telegram of condolence of Your Highness on the sorrowful martyrdom of the late Professor Mutahhari, the esteemed Islamic philosopher—may his soul be sanctified—has been received. I thank Your Highness for the expression of deep sympathy. I pray to the Almighty God for the glory of Islam and Muslims, and the severance of the hands of the outsiders and enemies of religion.

---

[32] *Ibid.*, p. 241.
[33] Letter dated May 11, 1979 [Ordibehesht 21, 1358 AHS / Jamadi ath-Thani 14, 1399 AH]. *Ibid.*, p. 242.

Ruhullah   al-Musawi   al-Khomeini

Jamadi ath-Thani 15, 1399 AH[34]

While exposing the treason and contradictory stances of the claimants of human rights, in a speech delivered to members of the Iranian Chamber of Commerce on May 15, 1979 [Ordibehesht 25, 1358 AHS/Jamadi ath-Thani 18, 1399 AH], the Imam mentioned the case of Mutahhari in this fashion:

Those like Mr. Mutahhari who would not hurt a fly—I knew this man for approximately twenty years—a man of such morality, a man of such grace, of such humanity was condemned to assassination.

Why? What had Mutahhari done? Whom had he killed? What was his crime? Was he not a human being? This man of philosophy, knowledge, religious scholar, and scientist—was he not a human being? They kill this human being in this fashion without having committed a single crime. What was the crime of Mr. Mutahhari? What had he done? What was the crime of Waliyyullah Qarani?[35] But what were they guilty of that they deserved to die?

Now too they have prepared a list of those who are to be assassinated. Are they under the mistaken impression that with the killing of Mr. Mutahhari or the killing of those like Mr. Mutahhari, this movement will die out and once again, the rights of our nation will be trampled upon? Once again, these human rights activists did not write a word about Mr. Mutahhari or say a word. At least we have not heard them utter a word. Was he not a human being? They did not protest, they said nothing; they did not condemn the person who killed him.

---

[34] Message dated May 12, 1979 [Ordibehesht 22, 1358 AHS/Jamadi ath-Thani 15, 1399 AH]. *Ibid.*, p. 247.

[35] Martyr Waliyyullah Qarani, first post-revolution Chief of Joint Staff of the Armed Forces.

Now they claim not to know him. Well, why did not they condemn the group who committed this act? Now, if we are to find Mutahhari's killer and punish him for his crime, in retribution, then they will raise their voice that it is an act of violence. Is it not violence to kill an innocent man for no reason? Sometimes, a person may have done something, whereas this man had no vocation other than to teach and to study. He was a person whom I had known for about twenty years, and I was informed of his condition and status, and I know that he has not hurt any person; a man who had toiled for this nation; a man who was an author of books; a man who was a philosopher and an intellectual deserved to be killed that they assassinated him? Where are the human rights groups that they are not uttering a single word? Now, if we find the person who has killed him and sentence him to death, then all of a sudden, the pens of the human rights activists will begin to write and publicize it as an act of violence. That Iran is a violent country that does not respect human rights. What sort of a group are these people? I do not know what kind of an upbringing they have had; what sort of animals are they?[36]

Another telegram of condolence was replied by the Imam on May 16, 1979 [Ordibehesht 26, 1358 AHS/Jamadi ath-Thani 19, 1399 AH]:

In His Most Exalted Name

His Eminence Hujjat al-Islam wal-Muslimin Mr. Khadimi, may his blessings last:

Your telegram of condolence about the martyrdom of the late Hujjat al-Islam wal-Muslimin Professor Mutahhari has been duly received. Yet, another telegram on this occasion has been received from the respected business guilds and the rest of the strata of the people of Isfahan. Convey my profound thanks and greetings to all the respected gentlemen. I pray to the Blessed God for the success and happiness of all of you. May God's peace, mercy, and blessings be upon you.

---

[36] *Sahifeh-ye Imam*, vol. 7, p. 312.

On the same day (May 16, 1979 [Ordibehesht 26, 1358 AHS/Jamadi ath-Thani 19, 1399 AH]) the Imam delivered a speech to a group of residents and tribes of the city of Khorramabad, the capital of Lorestan province. Elsewhere in the speech, the Imam states:

Now that they have witnessed their defeat in the referendum—their convincing defeat—and felt the attraction of the nation to Islam; and tasted their own defeat, they have resorted to desperate actions; to desperate moves. They have assassinated our important personalities, and they perceive that with their assassinations, things will go their way. This assassination of martyr Murtada Mutahhari has proven that the more blood the people of Iran see and the more hardship they suffer, the stronger they become. The steely determination of our nation is not in a manner that you can defeat it with these desperate moves. Our nation has found its course, and now will not rest until it has implemented the beloved Islam, until it has chopped off the hands of all traitors, and until it has put a stop to the plunder of the parasites.[38]

In another speech on May 21, 1979 [Ordibehesht 31, 1358 AHS/Jamadi ath-Thani 24, 1399 AH] addressed to a number of students of the Faculty of Law, Tehran University, the Imam mentioned Mutahhari in this way:

We are obligated to do our best to safeguard this movement until its final establishment, in order to see empowerment of an Islamic government. We must establish a religious government that could be a model in the world, to show the foreigners what democracy is, what does freedom mean. They complain about lack of freedom and human rights

---

[37] *Ibid.*, p. 325.
[38] *Ibid.*, pp. 328-329.

violations in Iran because we detain and punish the assassins and thieves, but when the enemies kill influential people like Mr. Mutahhari, they remain silent.

We want to form a form of Islamic government to show them what human rights means, what freedom is, what the rights of women are, the rights of men, and the rights of farmers. We want to form such a thing if the satanic powers, the mercenaries of the Great Satan, do allow us to do so. Then, they will see how Islam respects the laborers, the farmers, religious minorities, and all strata of the people. However, they do not give us a chance to work on it. I wish all the best for you and for all strata of the people. I feel tired now, and at another opportunity, I will talk about it more.[39]

And before another group of students, on May 23, 1979 [Khordad 2, 1358 AHS/Jamadi ath-Thani 26, 1399 AH], the Imam talked of Mutahhari, thus:

You should make sure you find out what anybody under any name, any delegation under any title, any association under any name, and anybody who is making a lot of noise about being an expert in law says or puts down in his or their writings. Look at what they do when they get together, pay attention to the way they oppose Islam.40[38]. Make sure to find out what types of people make up these groups. They first try to insinuate themselves into our circles, but then they have nothing to say about Islam. Find out what types of groups are trying to leave the clergy out, as they killed the very clerics who had led the movement to victory at the beginning of the Constitutional Revolution. This is the very same conspiracy. In those days they assassinated Sayyid 'Abdullah Behbahani and the late Nuri,[41] and then they changed the course of the people's movement. It is that very

---

[39] *Ibid.*, pp. 415-416.
[40] Addressing a number of lawyers, Hasan Nazih, the Oil Minister of the Provisional Government after the Iranian Revolution stated that Islam was not capable of administering the society.
[41] Fadlullah Nūri.

same plot for which they killed Mutahhari today, and they may kill me tomorrow and kill somebody else the day after that.[42]

On the occasion of the assassination attempt on Mr. 'Ali-Akbar Hashimi Rafsanjani, part of the Imam's message dated May 26, 1979 [Khordad 5, 1358 AHS/Jamadi ath-Thani 29, 1399 AH] reads:

The Americans and other superpowers should learn that our nation is alive. The mass rallies staged in the past few days go a long way to prove that the Revolution is alive. These people can never kill our Revolution through their stupid approaches. They can never eliminate humane and Islamic personalities of Mutahhari and Hashimi through their terrorist acts. There is no denying the fact that these assassination attempts are premeditatedly calculated and well organized, while the telltale tracks of international and criminal superpowers in such crimes are easily discernable.[43]

On the same day of the issuance of the above message (May 26, 1979), the Imam emphasized to a group of women and families of students of the Qum seminary the fact that assassination of individuals such as Mutahhari is not synonymous with the assassination of the movement:

You are responsible; we are all responsible. God, the Blessed and Exalted, has entrusted everybody with this responsibility and has commanded in this noble verse: *"Allah is sufficient for you and (for) such of the believers that follow you."* God has made those who obeyed you—the Holy Prophet—of the pious believers, of the pious believers who are the followers of Islam, who are the followers of the Messenger of Islam; these individuals suffice the Prophet, the Messenger of God. There is one big responsibility on the shoulders of everyone; on all the followers; on the whole nation who is the follower of the Prophet, which is that the manifestation of this verse, *"Allah is sufficient for you and (for)*

---

[42] *Sahifeh-ye Imam*, vol. 7, p. 459.
[43] *Ibid.*, p. 495.

such of the believers that follow you" must be visible on their foreheads; they must safeguard the religion of God; they must protect Islam and the glorious Qur'an. That they should not submit to these feeble revolts that these inhuman individuals are creating in Iran; they should not be afraid that these weaker sections have joined these revolts, and by their wishful thinking assassinate personalities in order to terrorize the nation. The assassination of individuals is not the assassination of the movement. Our movement is perpetual, even in the absence of personalities such as the late Mutahhari and Mr. Hashimi[44] and others. God, the Blessed and Exalted, and the pious followers of the honorable Prophet are sufficient. The nation is sufficient. And our nation has discovered its path. There is no fear. We shall never be afraid of these assassinations; and we shall never retreat; and we shall never allow the East or the West to interfere in the affairs of our country.[45]

In an address to members of the Central Council of the Iran Statistics Center on June 10, 1979 [Khordad 20, 1358 AHS/Rajab 15, 1399 AH], the Imam cited the case of Mutahhari in exposing the collapse of moral standards and human principles in the West:

The West is totally unaware of this. The West is after manufacturing aircraft; it is not concerned with human beings. Man must make the world; the West has nothing to do with man. It is concerned with aircraft and such things. It is leading mankind toward destruction. It is bringing up people as savages and murderers. Those who kill the most and eat the most are savages. The West is bringing up human beings as savages; the type that kills and devours people! It is turning out savages.

Islam, on the other hand, brings up people that are friendly and considerate. Even when Islam went to war and

---

[44] Murtada Mutahhari was martyred by the terrorist group of Furqan on May 1, 1979, and after some time, Hashimi Rafsanjani was attacked, but it was not a successful one.

[45] *Sahifeh-ye Imam*, vol. 7, p. 504-5.

destroyed corrupt elements, it was out of its loving concern for society. As those people were corrupt, they (Islam's leaders) would destroy them in order to eradicate the cancerous tumor and to allow society to develop on the right lines. It is all a matter of loving concern. We are calling for the execution of these few corrupt people because they are like cancerous tumor, they are wicked. It is because they corrupt society, and have corrupted a society! Now that these corrupt ones are being executed, a clamor has arisen in the West over the executions. They (West) say that these people are their friends. Well, we are executing them for this very reason. They say, "These people are of us; they have helped us!" and so they are raising a hue and cry over our killing their lackeys. We are punishing them for this very reason, on these very grounds, of being your servants, of acting against our nation and Islam and of killing the people. Not a word was uttered, not a single word, when they assassinated the late (Ayatullah) Mutahhari! But they raised a hue and cry when Hoveyda[46] was executed.[47]

And on June 13, 1979 [Khordad 23, 1358 AHS / Rajab 18, 1399 AH], the Imam raised to a group of students from Tehran University the issue of the need to confront the conspirators in the university, as what Mutahhari did before:

---

[46] The person in question is Amir 'Abbas Hoveyda, the son of 'Abdul-Malik and the grandson of a well-known Baha'i in Iran. He was educated in Beirut and in 1944 [1323 AHS] was appointed as a foreign diplomat in the Ministry of Foreign Affairs. In 1960 [1339 AHS] he became a member of the board of directors in the National Iranian Oil Company and in 1964 [1343 AHS] the Finance Minister in Mansūr's Cabinet. He succeeded Mansūr as Prime Minister in 1965 [1344 AHS] and remained as such until the year 1977 [1356 AHS]. In 1979 [1358 AHS] he was tried and executed. He is believed to have been a follower of the Baha'i school. His grandfather, Mirza Rida Qannad, was one of the devout activists and supporters of 'Abbas Effendi, a leading figure of the Baha'i sect, and after fleeing Iran he went to 'Akka in Occupied Palestine where he served 'Abbas Effendi as his servant.

[47] *Sahifeh-ye Imam*, vol. 8, pp. 81-82.

Sir, are you sitting by to see some communists come and take over the university? Are you inferior to them in any way? You are greater in number; you have better credentials. You can expose their treachery by stating these facts in that place; in the university. You can reveal their treason so that they go away. Stand your ground and speak out. Tell them, Sir. Each one of you should ask them who they are to come into the university and create disturbances. Ask them what they are up to; do they want to teach you? Tell them to first consider as to what they are in this country. Ask them whether they belong to this country or are foreign agents out to trouble you. Stand firm, Sir, and speak out. The orators (preachers), of course, should also come to the university; I suggest that Mr. Sayyid ‘Ali Khamene’i[48] come. If possible, please go and tell him on my behalf to come in the place of Mr. Mutahhari. He is very good; he is intelligent; he can talk; he can express himself.[49]

In volume 9 of the anthology, in his speech to professors of the University of Isfahan and Islamic Association of employees of the Ministry of Interior on July 15, 1979 [Tir 24, 1358 AHS/Sha‘ban 1399 AH], the Imam highlighted the terrorist action of the splinter groups as repugnant to Islam and the interest of the nation:

We must ask a question from these people that some of these groups that create this chaos and regard themselves as Islamic or supporters of the people and the masses and so forth, that well, if you are Islamic and are Muslims, then how is it that your actions are contrary to Islam? The killing of a person who spent his life for the propagation of Islam; for attestation of the religion of Islam such as Martyr Mutahhari or making an attempt on the life of theologian whose life was spent in the service of Islam and no one had heard a thing from him that was contrary to the interest of Islam such as Mr.

---

[48] It refers to the present Supreme Leader of the Islamic Revolution, Āyatullah al-‘Uz)ma Sayyid ‘Ali Khamene’i.

[49] *Sahifeh-ye Imam*, vol. 8, p. 138.

Razi Shirazi who is now hospitalized, how do these acts conform to Islam? You claim that you are Muslims and wish to serve Islam whereas you attempt to assassinate the theologians of Islam and the progeny of the Messenger of Islam! If they belong to the group that says we are supporters of the masses and the people and so forth; I would like to say that in these five months that the Islamic Republic has been established have you seen anything except service to the people, have you seen the agents of the present government break into some persons' home and take away an innocent person? Except that they put on trial degenerate individuals, or those who slaughtered the people en masse or ordered killings. Do you not burn the cultivated lands of the people; do you not prevent them from cultivating the farmlands; and when they do cultivate, you prevent them from harvesting the produce; and when they have harvested, you burn the harvests; is this service to the nation? Is this service to the masses? This referendum in which 98 – 98.5% of the people voted in favor, if you want the good of the masses; if you have the interest of the people in mind, well then these people have wanted this regime so why are you indulging in acts of terrorism? What happened that some of you boycotted it? You burnt some of the ballot boxes and prevented some from voting at the point of a gun, are these in the interest of the masses? Now that they are serving the people; now that they are busy putting the house in order; now that they are busy clearing the house; now that the people are busy serving; you are creating disturbances in this fashion; are these in the interests of the people?[50]

And elsewhere in an interview granted to British Muslim journalists, and some African and Asian journalists on December 16, 1979 [Azar 25, 1358 AHS/Muharram 26, 1400 AH], the Imam repeated the splinter group's terrorist and sabotage acts' repugnance to Islam and the interests of the Iranian nation:

---

[50] *Ibid.*, vol. 9, p. 96.

Which one of us is the dictator? Which one of us acts democratically: you, who become brain-washed by others, or us who prepare two cased for people's voting? Everywhere in the world election is done once, we have done it twice. Is this dictatorship? You have seen that some group of people, captured the television network.[51] This group is called "The devoted guerrillas," whom everyone of you recognize, who martyred Mr. Mutahhari—may God bless him—who killed major general Qarani, who shot M. Hashemi[52] to assassinate him and who killed Mr. Qazi.[53] And you should see what sort of agitators have come together to further their cases of agitation.[54]

The Imam also mentioned of Mutahhari in explaining the impact of the assassination of the religious dignitaries and its aftermath in a speech to the champions of the freestyle wresting in the Asian tournaments as well as the champions of the ancient style wrestling on December 19, 1979 [Azar 28, 1358 AHS/Muharram 29, 1400 AH]:

I am surprised at the degree of the stupidity of these agitators. The assassination of personalities such as Mr. Mutahhari or Mr. Mufatteh is just an excuse in the hands of these troublemakers to weaken our Islamic movement. And their stupidity is even felt more when they see that people unite when a scholar like Mr. Mutahhari is assassinated. If after each assassination half of the people had withdrawn from their supporting Islam and the Islamic government, then they would have tried to assassinate another personality, such as Mr. Qadi or Mr. Mufattih, to let the other half of the population disperse. However, much of their astonishment, they have realized that after each assassination trial, the movement takes up more momentum, and is welcomed more by people. The reason for their miscalculation lies in the fact

---

[51] The occupation of radio and television at Tabriz.

[52] Mr. Akbar Hashemi Rafsanjani.

[53] Mr. Qadi Tabataba'i, the Friday Imam of Tabriz, who was assassinated by a terrorist group called Furqan.

[54] *Sahifeh-ye Imam*, vol. 11, p. 308.

that they are made blind and deaf of God. Allah has deprived them of their rightful thinking. They themselves are to blame for this deprivation. They have acted in such a way that they are deprived of the faculties of visualization and conceptualization. Now they are engaged in doing things contrary to their own interests.[55]

On December 23, 1979 [Dey 2, 1358 AHS / Safar 3, 1400 AH], the Imam stressed to the household of Martyr Mufatteh the invincibility of the Islamic Revolution notwithstanding the elimination of its key figures such as Mutahhari and Mufattih himself:

I hope no one else would get assassinated. They kill our dignitaries one by one in the hope to strike a blow over us. But after each assassination we will see the Revolution becomes warmer and takes on a momentum. When the late Mutahhari was taken from us, people did not sit idle. The same thing is happening not that Mr. Mufatteh is martyred. People now are different in that they would not quit even if they are confronted with many disasters. The enemy's efforts are in vain since our nation is invincible now. It is nonsense to threaten us with the military intervention. Suppose this happened, our country would not fear the military forces. A nation who took to the streets, resisting such a devilish government and brought it down would not get frightened even if the enemies brought about bloodshed.[56]

And in a speech on January 1, 1980 [Dey 11, 1358 AHS / Safar 12, 1400 AH] to a group of Women of Azerbaijan Province, the Imam said: "At that time, the Furqan group, for example, a group which is a terrorist, would assassinate such persons as Mr. Mutahhari, and announce it."[57]

In volume 12, the Imam issued a message to the Iranian nation on March 17, 1980 [Esfand 27, 1358 AHS/Rabi' ath-

---

[55] *Sahifeh-ye Imam*, vol. 11, p. 334.
[56] *Ibid.*, p. 392.
[57] *Ibid.*, p. 526.

Thani 29, 1400 AH], recommending the youth to read the books of Prof. Martyr Mutahhari. The full text of the message reads:

In the Name of God, the Compassionate, the Merciful

Although the Islamic Revolution of Iran has attained victory in spite of the ill-wishers and adventure-seeking elements, it was the will and pleasure of God. Organizations, Islamic and revolutionary, have come into being one after another. All this within a year, and in calm and with success. At the same time, great many losses—irreparable or irretrievable —hailed on our nation and on our academic and Islamic institutions at the hands of hypocrites and anti-revolutionaries. Similarly, the assassination of the scholar and specialist in Islam, His Eminence Hujjat al-Islam Hajj Shaykh Murtada Mutahhari, may God have mercy on him.

I cannot express my feelings and sentiments at this moment of sensation with regards to this dear one. The thing that I can tell about him is that he rendered much valuable services to Islam and learning. It a matter of sorrow that the traitors' hand has uprooted this fruit yielding tree from the institutes of leaning and Islam. They deprived all from the valuable fruits of the late professor. Mutahhari was a dear son to me and a strong backing to the religious and academic institutions. He was a useful servant to the nation and the country. May God bestow upon him mercy and host him along with the great servants of Islam.

Now it is being heard that the anti-Islamic and anti-revolutionary groups are canvassing propaganda (anti-Islamic) to keep our youth from reading the books of this professor. I recommend the students and the class of open-minded ones to not let the books of this scholar to be neglected. I wish success to all from God. Peace be upon the virtuous servants of God.

Ruhullah al-Musawi al-Khomeini
Esfand 27, 1358 AHS

On the question of the song versified on the occasion of the martyrdom of Mutahhari, the Imam has this to say before a group of IRIB personnel on June 16, 1980 [Khordad 25, 1359 AHS/Sha'ban 2, 1400 AH: "The songs which are useful and exciting can be broadcast. There is no objection to it. The song of Mr. Mutahhari has no objection."[59]

Volume 14 contains a message dated April 29, 1981 [Ordibehesht 9, 1360 AHS/Jamadi ath-Thani 24, 1401 AH] that Imam Khomeini issued on the occasion of the coming of Murtada Mutahhari's martyrdom anniversary. The full text of the message is as follows:

In the Name of God, the Compassionate, the Merciful

It is the martyrdom anniversary of Mutahhari who, in his short lifespan, has left immortal works which are a reflection of an awakened conscience and soul filled with love of the creed. With his versatile pen and a gifted mind in analyzing Islamic issues and explaining philosophical truth, and with the language (level of understanding) of the people and tranquil and tranquility-giving words, he engaged in teaching and educating the society. Without exception, his writings and speeches are all educational and life-giving. His preaching and admonition which emanated from a heart full of faith and conviction are beneficial and pleasant for both the gnostic [*'arif*] and the commoner [*'ami*]. It is hoped that from this fruitful tree, more than what have been left fruits of knowledge and faith would be picked up and valuable scholars be offered to the society. Unfortunately, the hand of the traitors did not give respite (as it assassinated him) and deprived our dear youth of the wholesome fruit of this fruitful tree. Thanks to God that what have been left by this martyred professor having rich substance are educational and instructive. The late martyred

---

[58] *Sahifeh-ye Imam*, vol. 12, pp. 187-188.
[59] *Ibid.*, p. 440.

Professor Murtada Mutahhari joined eternity. By His mercy, may his Lord include him in the company of his masters.

Ruhullah al-Musawi al-Khomeini[60]

In Volume 15, in a speech to families of the martyrs of the Tir 7 tragedy and members of the Central Office of the Islamic Republic Party on July 2, 1981 [Tir 11, 1360 AHS / Sha'ban 29, 1401 AH], the Imam exposed the aim of the enemy in eliminating devoted elements of the Revolution by citing the case of Mutahhari:

What is important for us is that we perform our duty; that which God, the Blessed and Exalted, has ordained, we will undertake. For those who have connection with God, the martyrdom of the dear ones does not matter; what matters is the service rendered by the dear ones. They have rendered their services and for this nation they were assets that were lost. However, the path that they trod we have to follow with consciousness. From the initial stage of the movement and from the early part of the Revolution, there was an existing trend opposing the Revolution. It was not just accidental that they martyred one after another influential individuals, individuals who were assets of this nation... It was not that ... a person would just assassinate the late Mutahhari, the late Mufattih, Mr. Hashimi, Mr. Khamene'i, the late Beheshti, or these ministers each of whom was precious for Islam, or those representatives who were devoted and important.[61]

Interestingly enough, in the same volume, there is a record of the memorial note of Mutahhari being offered by the Imam to his daughter-in-law, Fatimah Tabataba'i, on January 26, 1982 [Bahman 6, 1360 AHS/Rabi' al-Awwal 30, 1402 AH]. The memorial note reads:

In the Name of God, the Compassionate, the Merciful

---

[60] *Ibid.*, vol. 14, p. 325.

[61] *Sahifeh-ye Imam*, vol. 15, p. 23.

I do hereby give the memorial note of martyred thinker Mutahhari as my remembrance and memorial note to my dear daughter Fati—may God Almighty give her success. It is hoped that she would benefit as much as she can from the valuable books of our martyr and remember him in her benevolent prayers.[62]

Ruhullah al-Musawi al-Khomeini

Bahman 6, 1360 AHS
Rabi' al-Awwal 30, 1402 AH[63]

In a speech (May 1, 1982 [Ordibehesht 11, 1361 AHS / Rajab 7, 1402 AH]) to Ahmad Tawakkuli (the then Minister of Labor and Social Affairs) as well as workers of the industrial and production units of the country on the occasion of International Labor Day, which also falls on the death anniversary of the late Mutahhari, the Imam describes Mutahhari in these words:

Since the day corresponds to the death anniversary of the late Mutahhari—may Allah have mercy on him—I have to give a statement to you concerning him. The late Mr. Mutahhari was a person who embodied different aspects. The service that has been rendered by the late Mutahhari to the youth and others has been done by only a few. All the literary works he has are all excellent without exception. I know nobody about whom I could say that all his works without exception are excellent. Without any exception, all his works are excellent, gearing toward the molding of man. He has rendered service to the country. Amidst the state of suppression, this prominent man has done great services. By the truth of the Noble

---

[62] The memorial note of Martyr Murtada Mutahhari was compiled as the First Book under the supervision of Mr. 'Abdul-Karim Surush, a copy of which Imam Khomeini offered, with the above note written at its first page, to Fatimah Tabataba'i, the wife of Sayyid Ahmad Khomeini.

[63] *Sahifeh-ye Imam*, vol. 15, p. 523.

Messenger, may God include him in the company of the Noble Messenger...[64]

There is also a mention of Mutahhari in a very brief autobiography written by the Imam sometime in 1986 [1364 AHS / 1406 AH], i.e. two years before his spiritual ascension: "After his arrival (i.e. the arrival of Ayatullah Burujerdi in Qum), I had to teach jurisprudence in the highest level [*dars al-kharij*] upon the request of such gentlemen as the late Mr. Mutahhari..."[65]

Finally, in the last volume (volume 21), barely 10 months before his demise the Imam is reported to have made mention of the late Professor in a message dated September 5, 1988 [Shahrivar 14, 1367 AHS / Muharram 23, 1409 AH] to the Muslim nation of Pakistan; the *'ulama'* of Islam on the martyrdom of Sayyid 'Arif-Husayn Husayni:

And the Muslim nations definitely have realized the reason behind this incident, why in Iran "Mutahharis," "Beheshtis," martyrs of the altar, and other dear clerics, and in Iraq "Sadrs" and "Hakims," and in Lebanon 'Raghibharbs" and "Kurims," and in Pakistan "'Arif-Husaynis," and in all countries the clerics who well-acquainted with the pure Muhammadan Islam are the subject of conspiracy and terrorism.[66]

In sum, the following table shows the chronological instances of the Imam's direct communication with the late Ayatullah Mutahhari and mentioning of his name or description of his personality.

---

[64] *Ibid.*, vol. 16, p. 242.
[65] *Ibid.*, vol. 19, 427.
[66] *Ibid.*, vol. 21, p. 120.

Figure 2 *Sahifeh-ye Imam*'s Chronological Accounts of Mutahhari

Volume	Period	Files	Pages
1	March 1933 – October 23, 1965 [Farvardin 1312 – Aban 1, 1344 AHS]	List of Permissions	488
2	October 24, 1965 – September 7, 1973 [Aban 2, 1344 – Shahrivar 16, 1352 AHS]	Permission, Letter	221, 424
3	October 8, 1973 – October 13, 1978 [Mehr 16, 1352 – Mehr 21, 1357 AHS]	Letter	328
7	April 12 – May 29, 1979 [Farvardin 23 – Khordad 8, 1358 AHS]	Messages, Speeches, Letters, Statements	182-3, 194, 197, 202, 207-11, 219-21, 240, 242, 247, 249, 254, 301, 312, 325, 329, 459, 495, 505,
8	May 29 – July 9, 1979 [Khordad 8 – Tir 18, 1358 AHS]	Speeches	82, 149
9	July 8 – September 17, 1979 [Tir 17 – Shahrivar 26, 1358 AHS]	Speech	96
11	November 8, 1979 – January 2, 1980 [Aban 17 – Dey 12, 1358 AHS]	Interview, Speeches	308, 334, 392, 526
12	January 2, 1980 – July 6, 1980 [Dey 12, 1358 – Tir 15, 1359 AHS]	Message, Speech	187-188, 440
14	January 22 – June 29, 1981 [Bahman 2, 1359 – Tir 8, 1360 AHS]	Message	325
15	June 30, 1981 – January 26, 1982 [Tir 9 – Bahman 6, 1360 AHS]	Speech, Memorial Note	23, 523
16	January 30, 1982 – September 22, 1982 [Bahman 10, 1360 – Shahrivar 31, 1361 AHS]	Speech	242
19	August 5, 1984 – February 23, 1986 [Mordad 14, 1363 – Esfand 4, 1364 AHS]	Autobiography	427
21	March 21, 1988 – June 5, 1989 [Farvardin 1, 1367 – Khordad 15, 1368 AHS]	Speech	120

Sahifeh-ye Imam's Account of Mutahhari:
An Analytical Survey

A close scrutiny of the *Sahifeh-ye Imam*'s chronological and descriptive accounts of Mutahhari shows that the martyred Ayatullah Professor Murtada Mutahhari undoubtedly occupies a distinct station in the sight of the Great Leader of the Islamic Revolution and the Idol-Breaker of the 20th Century. In the words of Ayatullah Dr. Sayyid Muhammad Husayn Beheshti,

"I think the reason for the Imam to hold such Professor Mutahhari in such high esteem and respect was not only because the Professor had been a student of him, but more as a close friend. The Imam believed in his knowledge and virtues, and was confident of his way of thinking, and his discernment in all things."[67]

Imam Khomeini's communications with Ayatullah Mutahhari in the forms of religious permissions and personal letters, as well as descriptions of him in letters, speeches, messages, statements, interviews, autobiography, and memorial note during and after his lifetime as indicated in the encyclopedic authentic reference source suggest that the former considers the latter a trustworthy representative, compassionate teacher, erudite scholar, competent jurist, eloquent speaker, combatant *'alim*, and an epitome of martyrdom in the way of truth and freedom of thought. These benevolent views on him are consistent from the first volume of the anthology in which Professor Mutahhari is indicated having been granted authority [*ijazah*] on Dhu'l-Hijjah 24,

---

[67] "Prominent Figures Hail Mutahhari," *Tehran Times Special Issue on the Martyrdom Anniversary of Ayatullah Mutahhari*, May 1, 1997, p. 4.

1388 AHS (March 13, 1969) by the Imam in the financial and religious law affairs up to the 21st volume (volume 22 being the indexes of the whole voluminous treatise) wherein he—in the Imam's message dated Shahrivar 14, 1367 AHS (September 5, 1988) addressed to the Muslim nation of Pakistan and the *'ulama'* of Islam on the occasion of the martyrdom of Sayyid 'Arif Husayn Husayni—is mentioned as among "the freedom-loving *'ulama'* of the Islamic world subjected to conspiracy and terrorism".

As a trustworthy representative

According to the principles of Shi'ah jurisprudence [*fiqh*], any expenditure of the religious payments and management of the Islamic financial affairs during the period of occultation of the twelfth Imam is not authorized without the permission of a fully qualified jurist; so it has been customary for the *maraji' at-taqlid* to issue letters of authorization for the qualified persons. These authorizations are granted by persons who meet the criteria of authority of imitation [*marja'iyyah*] in terms of general qualifications, devoutness and commitment, or their qualification is certified by two just informed persons. In turn, the competent jurist [*marja'*] issues authorizations to his official representatives who are either the prominent and pious scholars or persons who were closely in contact with and known to him, or those others with written endorsement of the just informed persons.

An index of the religious authorizations issued by Imam Khomeini during the period of his stay in the holy city of Najaf at the end of Volume 1 indicates that Ayatullah Mutahhari, apart from being an official representative of the Imam in the financial and religious law affairs, belong to the first category of representatives—"the prominent and pious scholars or persons who were closely in contact with and known to him":

334. To: Hujjat al-Islam Mr. Haj Shaykh Murtada Mutahhari Khorasani, in Tehran
Recommender: *Renowned*
Scope of Authority: Financial; delivering a half

Date: Dhu'l-Hijjah 1388 AH[68]

As a close associate and confidant

Apart from being a trusted proxy in financial and religious law affairs, the Imam's personal letter to Ayatullah Mutahhari on the death of the latter's father[69] and another letter concerning the regrettable state of affairs in the religious seminary at that time exemplify that the latter is also a close associate and confidant of the former. The following lines reveal the depth of communication between the former who was then in Najaf, Iraq and the latter then residing in Tehran:

I would like to say that I have received your esteemed letter… Most of the topics that have been mentioned were and are under consideration… there is no remedy except that the gentlemen who are acceptable and who, with respect to knowledge, can be provided, stay in the seminaries and take hold of the initiative. You are in a better position to select these people… these digressions must be prevented in practice. This should be accomplished by the efforts of the concerned notables including yourself.[70]

As a beloved son and student

Being known and close to him for more than twenty years,[71] the late Mutahhari is a beloved son and student for the Imam:

I have lost a very beloved son and mourn for him, for he was among the personalities that were considered to be the achievement of my life. With the martyrdom of this honorable son… it is a blow dealt on the beloved Islam that nothing can

---

[68] *Sahifeh-ye Imam*, vol. 1, p. 488. Emphasis added. See the full text of the permission at *Sahifeh-ye Imam*, vol. 2, p. 221.

[69] *Ibid.*, vol. 3, p. 328.

[70] *Ibid.*

[71] "He was a person whom I had known for about twenty years, and I was informed of his condition and status, and I know that he has not hurt any person." *Sahifeh-ye Imam*, vol. 7, p. 312.

substitute… I have lost a beloved child who was a part of my being.[72]

Mutahhari was a dear son to me…[73]

"After his arrival (i.e. the arrival of Ayatullah Burujerdi in Qum), I had to teach jurisprudence in the highest level [*dars al-kharij*] upon the request of such gentlemen as the late Mr. Mutahhari…"[74]

This affection to a beloved son and student can also be discerned in the Imam's replies to the messages of condolence. [75] Equally, the Imam's offer of the memorial note of Mutahhari to his daughter-in-law is also revealing.[76]

As an outstanding author and man of knowledge

As his student for many years, Mutahhari is remarkably acknowledged by the Imam as an outstanding author and man of knowledge as the following quotations from the *Sahifeh-ye Imam* indicate:

I express my condolences and congratulations to Islam, to its exalted prophets, to the nation of Islam and in particular, to the combatant people of Iran for the sorrowful loss of the honorable… thinker, philosopher and esteemed *faqih* [jurist] the late Haj Shaykh Murtada Mutahhari—may his soul rest in peace… condolences on the martyrdom of a man who was peerless in Islamology and various Islamic studies and the glorious Qur'an studies… With the martyrdom of this immortal scholar… it is a blow dealt on the beloved Islam that nothing can substitute…[77]

---

[72] *Ibid.* p. 178.
[73] *Sahifeh-ye Imam*, vol. 12, 187-188.
[74] *Ibid.*, vol. 19, 427.
[75] *Sahife-ye Imam*, vol. 7, pp. 194, 197, 202, 207-210, 241, 247, 325.
[76] *Ibid.*, vol. 15, p. 523.
[77] *Ibid.*, vol. 7, p. 178.

I received the telegram of condolence of Your Excellency, which was transmitted on the sorrowful martyrdom of the late Hujjat al-Islam wal-Muslimin Professor Mutahhari. I thank you for the expression of your sympathy. The martyrdom of one of the greatest scholars of Islam was a loss for the world of Islam and all the Muslims.[78]

The telegram of condolence of Your Highness on the sorrowful martyrdom of the late Professor Mutahhari, the esteemed Islamic philosopher—may his soul be sanctified—has been received.[79]

He was... a man who was an author of books; a man who was a philosopher and an intellectual...[80]

Similar is the case of the treacherous assassination of the scholar and specialist in Islam, His Eminence Hujjat al-Islam Hajj Shaykh Murtada Mutahhari, may God have mercy on him... The thing that I can tell about him is that he rendered much valuable services to... learning. It a matter of sorrow that the traitors' hand has uprooted this fruit-yielding tree from the institutes of leaning... They deprived all from the valuable fruits of the late professor. Mutahhari was a strong backing to the religious and academic institutions... I recommend the students and the class of open-minded ones to not let the books of this scholar be neglected.[81]

It is the martyrdom anniversary of Mutahhari who, in his short lifespan, has left immortal works which are a reflection of an awakened conscience and soul filled with love of the creed. With his versatile pen and a gifted mind in analyzing Islamic issues and explaining philosophical truth... he engaged in teaching and educating the society. Without exception, his writings... are all educational and life-giving... It is hoped that from this fruitful tree, more than what have been left fruits of

---

[78] *Ibid.*, p. 202.
[79] *Ibid.*, p. 247.
[80] *Ibid.*, p. 312.
[81] *Ibid.*, vol. 12, 187-188.

knowledge and faith would be picked up and valuable scholars be offered to the society. Unfortunately, the hand of the traitors did not give respite (as it assassinated him) and deprived our dear youth of the wholesome fruit of this fruitful tree. Thanks to God that what have been left by this martyred professor having rich substance are educational and instructive.[82]

It is hoped that she (Fatimah Tabataba'i, Imam Khomeini's daughter-in-law) would benefit as much as she can from the valuable books of our martyr and remember him in her benevolent prayers.[83]

All the literary works he (Mutahhari) has are all excellent without exception… Without any exception, all his works are excellent, gearing toward the molding of man…[84]

As an eloquent speaker and combatant 'alim

Apart from being a man of the pen, the Imam has recognized the late Mutahhari as an eloquent speaker and combatant 'alim as substantiated by the following statements:

Condolence on the martyrdom of a personage…who struggled ferociously with deviations and perversions… Mutahhari, who was peerless in…the power of oratory, has departed and joined the exalted souls.[85]

The orators (preachers), of course, should also come to the university; I suggest that Mr. Sayyid 'Ali Khamene'i[86] come. If possible, please go and tell him on my behalf to come in the place of Mr. Mutahhari. He is very good; he is intelligent; he can talk; he can express himself.[87]

---

[82] *Ibid.*, vol. 14, p. 325.

[83] *Ibid.*, vol. 15, p. 523.

[84] *Ibid.*, vol. 16, p. 242.

[85] *Ibid.*, vol. 7, p. 178.

86 It refers to the present Supreme Leader of the Islamic Revolution, Āyatullah al-'Uz)ma Sayyid 'Ali Khamene'i.

[87] *Sahifeh-ye Imam*, vol. 8, p. 138.

With the language (level of understanding) of the people and tranquil and tranquility-giving words, he engaged in teaching and educating the society. Without exception, his ... speeches are all educational and life-giving. His preaching and admonition which emanated from a heart full of faith and conviction are beneficial and pleasant for both the gnostic ['arif] and the commoner ['ami].[88]

And the Muslim nations definitely have realized the reason behind this incident, why in Iran "Mutahharis," "Beheshtis," martyrs of the altar, and other dear clerics, and in Iraq "Sadrs" and "Hakims," and in Lebanon "Raghibharbs" and "Kurims," and in Pakistan "'Arif-Husaynis," and in all countries the clerics who well-acquainted with the pure Muhammadan Islam are the subject of conspiracy and terrorism.[89]

As a dedicated and pious servant of Islam and the nation

In terms of general service to the people and religion, in the view of the Imam, Mutahhari is a dedicated and pious servant of Islam and the nation as he said:

Condolence on the martyrdom of a personage who spent his noble and precious life in the cause of the sacred objectives of Islam... Mutahhari who was peerless in purity of soul and strength of faith... has departed and joined the ranks of the exalted souls.[90]

He was a man who had toiled for this nation...[91]

[Mutahhari is] a person who spent his life for the propagation of Islam... a theologian whose life was spent in the service of

---

[88] *Ibid.*, vol. 14, p. 325.
[89] *Ibid.*, vol. 21, p. 120.
[90] *Ibid.*, vol. 7, pp. 178.
[91] *Ibid.*, p. 312.

Islam and no one had heard a thing from him that was contrary to the interest of Islam...[92]

The thing that I can tell about him is that he rendered much valuable services to Islam... It a matter of sorrow that the traitors' hand has uprooted this fruit yielding tree from Islam... He was a useful servant to the nation and the country.[93]

The service that has been rendered by the late Mutahhari to the youth and others has been done by only a few... He has rendered service to the country. Amidst the state of suppression, this prominent man has done great services...[94]

As an epitome of martyrdom and self-sacrifice, and reviver of the movement

In many instances, the Imam highlighted the point that Shahid Mutahhari is an epitome of martyrdom and self-sacrifice, as well as a reviver of the movement:

And felicitations on the possession of these self-sacrificing personalities who spread and are spreading light with their appearance, both in this life and the hereafter... who with their luminous light give life to the dead and spread light in darkness... They (the enemies) should know that by the will of the powerful God, with the departure of great individuals our nation will become more determined in its resolve to fight against immorality, tyranny, and oppression... The beloved Islam proliferated with the sacrifice and martyrdom of its most beloved ones. From the age of revelation until now, Islam has thrived on martyrdom interlaced with moral heroism.[95]

Our movement was resurrected. All sections of the people of Iran started life all over again. If it had developed lethargy or a weakness, it was resurrected. Was it not because of the martyrdom of this great man (Mutahhari); and had this great

---

[92] *Ibid.*, vol. 9, p. 96.
[93] *Ibid.*, vol. 12, 187-188.
[94] *Ibid.*, vol. 16, p. 242.
[95] *Ibid.*, pp. 178-179.

man died in his bed; this would not have been substantiated; this wave would not have arisen. Now a wave, all over the world; the entire world; all the world that is interested in Islam has arisen.[96]

...we must give such martyrs, for the cause of Islam. From day one when Islam was born, it has propagated this righteous religion with martyrdom. Islam has had great martyrs and it is honored to have given great martyrs in the way of God and in the path of its objective. We too are honored to give martyrs in the cause of Islam and in the path of our objective—and this man is not the last of our martyrs. We may again have to give martyrs...[97]

This Islam has been founded in this manner right from its inception and it has marched forward while giving martyrs; it has constantly given martyrs and moved forward. It was the same in the era of the Holy Prophet too. In the Battle of Uhud, so many people were killed and in the other battles, so many Muslims were killed but they were not worried at all. They would give martyrs and move one step forward; again they would give martyrs and move one step forward; And, praise be to God, now the situation is such that by giving a single martyr an upsurge is created all over Iran and outside Iran. Outside Iran also, the incident of the death of the late Mr. Mutahhari—which justifiably was a great loss for us and for the whole of Iran—as you are aware was a loss too, they broadcast on the radio stations that in Pakistan or in such and such place—everywhere—it has created a wave. These people too are making a mistake by killing Mr. Mutahhari. They must understand that the question is not that with the killing of a single person the people will retreat, when one is killed the whole lot comes forward and their cry becomes louder; the disgrace of the enemy also becomes more. And I hope that this spirit stays with us and with our nation.[98]

---

[96] *Ibid.*, p. 183-184.
[97] *Ibid.*, vol. 7, p. 197.
[98] *Sahifeh-ye Imam*, vol. 7, pp. 219-220.

Today, that you have gathered here to express your condolences on the death of one of our beloved, and for the assassination of a scholar, knowingly and determinedly you are resolved to continue the struggle against the *taghuti* regime, colonialism, and arrogance. My brothers! My sisters! My dear ones! Be resolute, do not be afraid of assassination; do not be afraid of martyrdom, and for sure you are not. Martyrdom is an eternal honor; it is immortality.[99]

This assassination of martyr Murtada Mutahhari has proven that the more blood the people of Iran see and the more hardship they suffer, the stronger they become. The steely determination of our nation is not in a manner that you can defeat it with these desperate moves. Our nation has found its course, and now will not rest until it has implemented the beloved Islam, until it has chopped off the hands of all traitors, and until it has put a stop to the plunder of the parasites.[100]

The Americans and other superpowers should learn that our nation is alive. The mass rallies staged in the past few days go a long way to prove that the Revolution is alive. These people can never kill our Revolution through their stupid approaches. They can never eliminate humane and Islamic personalities of Mutahhari and Hashimi through their terrorist acts.[101]

The assassination of personalities such as Mr. Mutahhari or Mr. Mufatteh is just an excuse in the hands of these troublemakers to weaken our Islamic movement. And their stupidity is even felt more when they see that people unite when a scholar like Mr. Mutahhari is assassinated. If after each assassination half of the people had withdrawn from their supporting Islam and the Islamic government, then they would have tried to assassinate another personality, such as Mr. Qadi or Mr. Mufatteh, to let the other half of the population disperse. However, much of their astonishment, they have

---

[99] *Ibid.*, p. 241.
[100] *Ibid.*, pp. 328-329.
[101] *Ibid.*, p. 495.

realized that after each assassination trial, the movement takes up more momentum, and is welcomed more by people.[102]

They kill our dignitaries one by one in the hope to strike a blow over us. But after each assassination we will see the Revolution becomes warmer and takes on a momentum. When the late Mutahhari was taken from us, people did not sit idle. The same thing is happening not that Mr. Mufatteh is martyred. People now are different in that they would not quit even if they are confronted with many disasters. The enemy's efforts are in vain since our nation is invincible now.[103]

As a furqan [criterion and acid test]
Viewing Mutahhari as with the truth and the truth with Mutahhari, the Imam considered him a *furqan* [criterion and acid test]. For example, for him, the assassination of Mutahhari is a standing criterion that distinguishes those who are really serving Islam and the people, on one hand, and those who saboteurs and conspirators aiming to uproot the religion:

Now that they have witnessed their defeat in the referendum—their convincing defeat—and felt the attraction of the nation to Islam; and tasted their own defeat, they have resorted to desperate actions; to desperate moves. They have assassinated our important personalities, and they perceive that with their assassinations, things will go their way. This assassination of martyr Murtada Mutahhari has proven that the more blood the people of Iran see and the more hardship they suffer, the stronger they become.[104]

Make sure to find out what types of people make up these groups. They first try to insinuate themselves into our circles, but then they have nothing to say about Islam. Find out what types of groups are trying to leave the clergy out, as they killed

---

[102] *Sahifeh-ye Imam*, vol. 11, p. 334.
[103] *Ibid.*, p. 392.
[104] *Sahifeh-ye Imam*, vol. 7, p. 329.

the very clergies who had led the movement to victory at the beginning of the Constitutional Revolution. This is the very same conspiracy. In those days they assassinated Sayyid 'Abdullah Behbahani and the late Nuri,[105] and then they changed the course of the people's movement. It is that very same plot for which they killed Mutahhari today, and they may kill me tomorrow and kill somebody else the day after that.[106]

We must ask a question from these people that some of these groups that create this chaos and regard themselves as Islamic or supporters of the people and the masses and so forth, that well, if you are Islamic and are Muslims, then how is it that your actions are contrary to Islam? The killing of a person who spent his life for the propagation of Islam; for attestation of the religion of Islam such as Martyr Mutahhari or making an attempt on the life of theologian whose life was spent in the service of Islam and no one had heard a thing from him that was contrary to the interest of Islam...[107]

Which one of us is the dictator? Which one of us acts democratically: you, who become brain-washed by others, or us who prepare two cased for people's voting? Everywhere in the world election is done once, we have done it twice. Is this dictatorship? You have seen that some group of people, captured the television network.[108] This group is called "The devoted guerrillas," whom everyone of you recognize, who martyred Mr. Mutahhari—may God bless him—who killed major general Qarani, who shot M. Hashemi to assassinate him and who killed Mr. Qazi. And you should see what sort of agitators have come together to further their cases of agitation.[109]

In the same vein, according to the Imam, the figure of Mutahhari also exposes that hypocrisy and fallacy of those

---

[105] Fadlullah Nuri.
[106] *Sahifeh-ye Imam*, vol. 7, p. 459.
[107] *Ibid.*, vol. 9, p. 96.
[108] The occupation of radio and television at Tabriz.
[109] *Sahifeh-ye Imam*, vol. 11, p. 308.

self-proclaimed defenders of democracy, human rights and freedom of thought:

Once again, these human rights activists did not write a word about Mr. Mutahhari or say a word. At least we have not heard them utter a word. Was he not a human being? They did not protest, they said nothing; they did not condemn the person who killed him. Now they claim not to know him. Well, why did not they condemn the group who committed this act? Now, if we are to find Mutahhari's killer and punish him for his crime, in retribution, then they will raise their voice that it is an act of violence. Is it not violence to kill an innocent man for no reason? ... Where are the human rights groups that they are not uttering a single word? Now, if we find the person who has killed him and sentence him to death, then all of a sudden the pens of the human rights activists will begin to write and publicize it as an act of violence.[110]

We must establish a religious government that could be a model in the world, to show the foreigners what democracy is, what does freedom mean. They complain about lack of freedom and human rights violations in Iran because we detain and punish the assassins and thieves, but when the enemies kill influential people like Mr. Mutahhari, they remain silent.[111]

They (West) say that these people are their friends. Well, we are executing them for this very reason. They say, "These people are of us; they have helped us!" and so they are raising a hue and cry over our killing their lackeys. We are punishing them for this very reason, on these very grounds, of being your servants, of acting against our nation and Islam and of killing the people. Not a word was uttered, not a single word, when they assassinated the late (Ayatullah) Mutahhari! But they raised a hue and cry when Hoveyda was executed.[112]

---

[110] *Sahifeh-ye Imam*, vol. 7, p. 312.
[111] *Sahifeh-ye Imam*, vol. 7, p. 416.
[112] *Sahifeh-ye Imam*, vol. 8, pp. 81-82.

As a multi-dimensional and exceptional figure

Mutahhari's multi-dimensionality and exceptional figure has not also escaped from the Imam's notice. In his words,

[t]he late Mr. Mutahhari was a person who embodied different aspects. The service that has been rendered by the late Mutahhari to the youth and others has been done by only a few. All the literary works he has are all excellent without exception. I know nobody about whom I could say that all his works without exception are excellent. Without any exception, all his works are excellent, gearing toward the molding of man. He has rendered service to the country. Amidst the state of suppression, this prominent man has done great services. By the truth of the Noble Messenger, may God include him in the company of the Noble Messenger...[113]

---

[113] *Ibid.*, vol. 16, p. 242.

Conclusion

From the foregoing, it can be deduced that based on reliable and authentic works and documents as recorded in *Sahifeh-ye Imam*, the Great Leader of the Islamic Revolution has benevolent views of Ayatullah Shaykh Murtada Mutahhari, and that these favorable views had been consistent from their acquaintanceship up to the time after Mutahhari's martyrdom.

For the Imam, Shahid Mutahhari is more than a trusted representative, close associate and confidant, beloved son and student, outstanding author and man of knowledge, eloquent speaker and combatant *'alim*, dedicated and pious servant of Islam and the nation, and a personification of martyrdom and self-sacrifice, as well as reviver of the movement. Indeed, it can be said that for him, Mutahhari cannot be confined to a single dimension as he is an embodiment of a totality. Mutahhari is Mutahhari.

About the Author

Mansoor Limba is a writer, translator, university professor, chess trainer, and blogger. He is a PhD holder in International Relations and BA holder in Islamic Studies who writes and translates books (Persian into English and Filipino, English into Filipino) on such subjects as international politics, history, political philosophy, intra-faith and interfaith relations, cultural heritage, Islamic finance, jurisprudence (*fiqh*), scholastic theology (*'ilm al-kalam*), Qur'anic sciences, hadith, ethics, and mysticism. Have an experience with his multidisciplinary taste by visiting his personal blog at http://www.mlimba.com and financial literacy website at https://www.muslimandmoney.com.

✓ The Radiance of the Secrets of Prayer
✓ The Qur'an as Reflected in Nahj al-Balaghah
✓ In the Presence of the Beloved: Commentaries on Du'a' al-Iftitah, Du'a' Abu Hamzah al-Thumali and Du'a' Makarim al-Akhlaq
✓ A Commentary on Prayer
✓ A Cursory Glance at the Theory of Wilayat al-Faqih
✓ Training and Education in Islam
✓ The Theory of Knowledge: An Islamic Perspective
✓ Islamic Political Theory, Volume 1 (Legislation)
✓ Islamic Political Theory, Volume 2 (Statecraft)
✓ Investigations and Challenges: Discourses on Current Cultural, Sociopolitical and Religious Issues
✓ An Introduction to Hadith: History and Sources
✓ Introduction to the Sciences of the Qur'an
✓ The Qur'an and Immunity from Distortion
✓ Discursive Theology, Volume 1
✓ Discursive Theology, Volume 2
✓ Philosophy of Religion
✓ Fitrah: Man's Natural Disposition
✓ Philosophy of Ethics
✓ Hijab and Mental Health
✓ Risalah Liqa' Allah: A Treatise on the Stages of Mystical Wayfaring toward the Station of Beatific Vision
✓ The Revival of Islamic Thought
✓ Risalah Ma'rifat Allah: An Exposition of Imam 'Ali ibn Musa al-Rida's ('a) Sermon on the Gnosis of Allah
✓ Misbah al-Shari'ah: A Commentary on Misbah al-Shari'ah (Lantern of the Path) Attributed to Imam Ja'far al-Sadiq (*a*)
✓ Esoteric Traditions: An Exposition of Imam Musa ibn Ja'far's (*a*) Mystical and Philosophical Traditions

- ✓ Imam al-Rida's (*'a*) Esoteric Traditions: An Exposition of Selected Traditions from *'Uyun Akhbar al-Rida*
- ✓ *Risalah Sayr wa Suluk*: An Exposition of Sayyid Bahr al-'Ulum's Treatise on Mystical Wayfaring
- ✓ Scientific Approach in Translating and Interpreting the Noble Qur'an and Traditions
- ✓ *Tafsir-e Rushan*: An Elucidated Exegesis of the Qur'an, Volume 1

Connect with Mansoor Limba

I really appreciate you reading my book! Here are my social media coordinates:

Friend me on Facebook:
https://www.facebook.com/mansoor.limba

Follow me on Twitter:

https://www.twitter.com/mansoor_limba

Follow me on Instagram:

https://www.instagram.com/m_limba

Pin my photos: https://www.pinterest.ph/mansoorlimba

Favorite my Smashwords author page:

https://www.smashwords.com/profile/view/mlimba

Favorite my Amazon author page:

http://www.amazon.com/author/mansoorlimba

Connect on LinkedIn:

https://ph.linkedin.com/pub/mansoor-limba/b6/383/720

Subscribe to my blog: http://www.mlimba.com

Subscribe to my channel:

http://www.youtube.com/c/wayfaringwithmansoor

Visit my financial literacy website:

https://www.muslimandmoney.com

Purchase my books: https://www.elzistyle.com